Whoopie Pies!

Whoopie Pies!

25 IRRESISTIBLE CAKE CREATIONS

MOWIE KAY

LORENZ BOOKS

This edition is published by
Lorenz Books, an imprint of
Anness Publishing Ltd
108 Great Russell Street
London WC1B 3NA

info@anness.com

www.lorenzbooks.com
www.annesspublishing.com

If you like the images in this book
and would like to investigate using
them for publishing, promotions or
advertising, please visit our website
www.practicalpictures.com for
more information.

© Anness Publishing Ltd 2014

A CIP catalogue record for this book is
available from the British Library.

Publisher: Joanna Lorenz
Editor: Kate Eddison, Helen Sudell
Photographer: Nicki Dowey
Food Stylist: Lucy McKelvie
Prop Stylist: Wei Tang
Designer: Lisa Tai
Production Controller: Rosanna Anness

COOK'S NOTES

- Bracketed terms are intended for American readers.
- For all recipes, quantities are given in both metric and imperial measures and, where appropriate, in standard cups and spoons. Follow one set of measures, but not a mixture, because they are not interchangeable.
- Standard spoon and cup measures are level. 1 tsp = 5ml, 1 tbsp = 15ml, 1 cup = 250ml/8fl oz.
- Australian standard tablespoons are 20ml. Australian readers should use 3 tsp in place of 1 tbsp for measuring small quantities.
- American pints are 16fl oz/2 cups. American readers should use 20fl oz/2.5 cups in place of 1 pint when measuring liquids.
- Electric oven temperatures in this book are for conventional ovens. When using a fan oven, the temperature will probably need to be reduced by about 10–20°C/20–40°F. Since ovens vary, you should check with your manufacturer's instruction book for guidance.
- The nutritional analysis given for each recipe, unless otherwise stated, is calculated per portion (i.e. serving or item).
  The analysis does not include optional ingredients, such as salt added to taste.
- Medium (US large) eggs are used unless otherwise stated.

PUBLISHER'S NOTE

Previously published as part of a larger volume, *Whoopie Pies*.

Contents

Introduction

Whoopie pies are considered to be an American creation, created to use up leftover cake mixture. It is thought that when the Amish found one of these treats in their lunch boxes, they would shout 'whoopie!' True or not, the name is now famous worldwide.

What is a whoopie pie?

Shaped like a burger, bigger and easier to make than macarons, and rapidly taking over from the cupcake as the kings of the baking world, whoopie pies are here to stay. A whoopie pie, at its most basic level, consists of two round 'cakes' that are sandwiched together with a deliciously soft filling. They can be flavoured with an endless array of ingredients, and then decorated with all sorts of toppings, from melted chocolate and runny honey to creamy icings and dustings of cocoa powder.

The original and best-known whoopie pie is wonderful in its simplicity: rich chocolate cakes with sticky marshmallow filling. Today, however, the range of cakes, fillings and toppings is seemingly infinite, demonstrating the versatility of this scrummy treat, and lending itself to mixing and matching cakes, fillings and toppings.

The cake mixture tends to be made using milk or buttermilk, and each whoopie pie maker has his or her preferences. In this book, buttermilk is the main liquid ingredient in the cakes as it results in a superior flavour, as well as making the cakes stay moist for longer. Buttermilk adds a richness to the whoopie pie cakes that you don't get in a simple cupcake.

All kinds of whoopie pies

Whoopie pies can be made in an almost limitless medley of flavours, sizes, shapes and colours. The original and standard whoopie pie is large enough to eat with two hands, as if biting into a burger. Once you have mastered making a basic whoopie, you can experiment with pretty much every aspect of the recipe. Try making them into mini whoopies or even into a giant whoopie cake! Fillings include, but

Above: Coloured icings, melted chocolate and pretty decorations give extra character to your whoopie pie creations.

Above: Make a batch of mini whoopie pies and stack them together to form a birthday cake pyramid.

are not limited to, marshmallow, buttercream and whipped cream, and each one can be augmented with sumptuous colours and intriguing flavours. Create your own special occasion whoopies by going to town on toppings: drizzle them decadently with chocolate, decorate them beautifully with icing, or brush them with an elegant fruity glaze.

Storing whoopie pies

Whoopie pies are generally best served on the day you make them, but they can be made in advance. Although moist when initially baked, the cakes can dry out very quickly if not stored correctly. You can make both the cakes and fillings ahead of when you need them, if you like, and store them both separately until you are ready to assemble. Alternatively, just make the cakes a day earlier and make the filling fresh on the day of serving.

To allow them to retain their moisture, wrap the whoopies in clear film (plastic wrap) or store them in an airtight container for up

to 5 days. If the filling has fresh cream in it, you will need to store them in the refrigerator for up to 2–3 days. For marshmallow and other fillings that do not need to be chilled, store them in an airtight container for up to 5 days. Once you are ready to serve them, bring any chilled whoopies to room temperature, then add the topping and decorations of your choice and serve immediately.

Above: Varied sizes of whoopie pie are suitable for different occasions. Any recipe can be adapted to make either mini, regular or large pies.

Whoopie pie sizes

The standard-sized whoopie pies are big enough to hold in both hands like a burger. The cakes are piped on to baking sheets in 5cm/2in rounds, but they can spread in the oven depending on the type of cake mixture. Mini whoopies are piped into 3cm/1¼in rounds and require roughly half the mixture for each cake. Therefore, the same recipe will make double the amount of minis.

You can also make a giant whoopie pie cake, perfect for birthdays, using a 24cm/9½in cake tin (pan) as a guide. The same amount of mixture will make 1 giant whoopie, 12 regular whoopies or 24 mini whoopies, so it is simple to adapt the recipes to make whichever size you require. Mini whoopie pie cakes will need a reduced cooking time, and giant cakes will need a bit longer in the oven.

Whoopie-making Equipment

You only need a few essentials to start baking whoopie pies; the rest you can acquire as you get more experienced. If you do get bitten by the whoopie pie bug try to invest in good quality equipment, if you can, as you will reap the benefits over time.

Baking tray Most ovens already come with a baking tray, but it is best to invest in at least one good quality baking tray that is flat and not curved at the edge. A good baking tray diffuses heat equally across its surface. If you cannot fit all the cakes on your baking trays, cook them in batches.

Baking parchment Used for lining baking trays, baking parchment is inexpensive. You can also buy siliconized baking parchment,which is silicone-coated on both sides, and provides a perfect non-stick surface for baking without having to grease trays or parchment. You can re-use it, so it is worth the extra expense.

Silicone mats Made from fibreglass and silicone, these mats can be used instead of baking parchment and can be re-used thousands of times. To clean, simply wash them in soapy water, rinse and allow them to dry. They save time and, in the long run, money, and are environmentally friendly as they create less waste.

Piping bags and nozzles Made of plastic, fabric or polyester, piping bags are the ultimate tool in achieving smooth, round whoopie pie cakes. With a bit of practice, you'll be piping perfect rounds with ease. Most bags are re-usable and fit a range of nozzles. Large, plain round nozzles are best for piping cake mixture (batter) on to baking trays. Smaller, star-shaped nozzles are useful for piping filling and decorating the tops.

Whoopie pie tins (pans) A new invention, whoopie pie tins are available in most baking stores. They were created solely for making whoopie pies. They are a simple, practical idea, which work as a great alternative to piping. They create evenly sized whoopie pies with very straight edges, so although they help you to make

Above: Piping bags are the best way to achieve pretty effects.

Above: An electric whisk makes beating cake mixtures an easy task.

Above: A palette knife will help you create a smoother topping when decorating your whoopie pies.

uniform cakes, they do not give the characteristic slopes of the classic whoopie.

Ice cream scoops Due to the thick consistency of whoopie pie cake mixture, an ice cream scoop can be the most practical way of making whoopie pie cakes. Hemispherical in shape, some are fitted with a mechanical release that drops a perfect round of cake mixture on to the baking trays, and are invaluable for nutty cake mixtures.

Electric food mixer A really important piece of equipment that allows you to mix and add ingredients hands-free, an electric food mixer is a time-saving investment that should last many years. It is also useful for making marshmallow filling. If you do not have one, a mixing bowl and an electric hand whisk will do.

Electric hand mix Useful in combination with an electric food mixer, an electric hand whisk allows you to make fillings at the same time as the cake mixtures are combining in the food mixer. This is also perfect for making buttercreams and whipping cream. Although more labour-intensive, a balloon whisk can be used instead.

Scales It is best to invest in digital scales for achieving precise measurements.

Sieve (strainer) This is essential for sifting flour into cake mixtures and for sifting icing (confectioners') sugar or cocoa powder when making smooth icings. Keep two separate ones for dry and wet ingredients.

Pastry brush Useful for brushing glazes on to the tops of whoopies, pastry brushes are available in many types, shapes and sizes. Silicone brushes are a good choice as they withstand

Above: Allow whoopie pie cakes to cool completely on a wire rack before filling and decorating.

heat, rinse easily and last much longer, with the added bonus of not losing any bristles.

Cooling racks When whoopie pie cakes come out of the oven, allow to cool on a wire rack.

Palette knife or metal spatula These tools are perfect for smoothing or creating peaks in icing or buttercream. Palette knives and metal spatulas are also useful for transferring baked whoopie pie cakes from baking trays on to cooling racks.

Pastry (cookie) cutters It is easy to form different whoopie pie shapes by pouring the cake mixture into a Swiss roll tin (jelly roll pan), baking it, then using pastry cutters to cut out shapes.

Tips and Techniques

There are a few techniques to get to grips with when making whoopie pies, such as decorative piping and making marshmallow filling, but once you have mastered a few tricks of the trade, you will be whipping up whoopies time and time again.

Preparing the cake mixture (batter)

The whoopie pie cake mixture is quite a forgiving and versatile batter that allows for small changes and mistakes; a little more or less flour or buttermilk won't ruin it. The quickest way to make the cake mixture is to use an electric food mixer, though you must fold in the dry ingredients by hand. You can always make the

Above: Piping whoopie pie cakes is a skill that can be mastered easily with a little practice.

cake mixture using an electric hand whisk, or a simple wooden spoon. The mixture should have a thick consistency: when a spatula in the mixture is lifted, the batter should tear with clear-cut edges. If the mixture drips off the spatula, it is too runny and you will need to add more flour.

Forming the cakes

You should be able to fit 12 regular-sized whoopie pie cakes on to each baking tray, but if not, just use more baking trays. Bake them in batches, if you need to. It is important to space the cakes 5cm/2in apart as once placed in the oven, the batter expands rapidly. The recipes in this book use a piping bag to form the cakes, but there are multiple ways of doing this such as using an ice cream scoop, pastry (cookie)

cutters or a whoopie pie tin (pan). The important thing is to achieve evenly sized whoopies to give that smooth professional finish.

Baking times and temperatures

When it comes to any form of baking, the best advice is to know your oven. Oven temperatures vary from one oven to the next, and temperatures within each

Above: For a simple , fuss-free method, form your whoopie pie cakes using an ice cream scoop.

Above: Melt chocolate over a pan of gently simmering water, if possible, stirring it until it is smooth.

oven vary from top to bottom, depending on the origin of heat. An oven thermometer is a very good investment. Place this on the same level as the baking tray before the baking tray goes into the oven to get an accurate reading. It is also best to clear the ovens of all baking trays and racks while preheating and baking, and to only have the trays of whoopie pies in the oven during baking. This helps heat distribution and reduces oven preheating times.

The bigger the whoopie pie cakes, the longer they need to bake. For the minis, this is around 10–12 minutes, for the normal size it is around 12–15 minutes,

and for the giant cakes it is between 20–30 minutes. The best way to test if a cake is ready is to press it gently. If it bounces back, it is ready to take out of the oven; if it doesn't bounce back it means it is still raw in the middle, and if it doesn't give when pressed, then it has been in too long.

Making marshmallow fillings

The classic marshmallow filling appears in many recipes and is surprisingly easy to make. It is best to use an electric food mixer to make it, but you can use a mixing bowl and an electric hand whisk if

Making buttermilk

Buttermilk is readily available in supermarkets, but if you cannot find it, an effective substitute can be made by adding 15ml/ 1 tbsp lemon juice to 250ml/ 8fl oz/1 cup full cream (whole) milk. Stir, then allow the mixture to stand for 5 minutes before using.

Above: It takes a bit of practice to get to grips with sticky marshmallow filling, but the results are worth it.

you do not have one. The mixture is too thick and sticky to use a balloon whisk. Due to its stickiness, piping can be difficult and messy, so spooning it on to the cakes is usually the better option.

Use two tablespoons, one to scoop up the mixture and the other to scrape it onto the whoopie base. Grease your spoons with a little vegetable oil to prevent the marshmallow from sticking. It is advisable to spoon the fresh marshmallow mixture on to the cakes straight away, as the gelatine starts to set once left to stand. You can always buy marshmallow fluff, for an instant marshmallow, if you like.

Whoopie Pie Recipes

If you are fond of eating cakes then you will find the following selection of whoopie pies irresistible. They are a treat with a pot of steaming tea or frothy coffee and are perfect for a quick afternoon pick-me-up. All the classic flavour combinations are here but there are also some decadent ideas to try. These whoopie pies are sure to impress your friends and will taste sensational.

The Classic Whoopie Pie

This is the original and classic whoopie pie recipe – two rich chocolate cakes sandwiched together with a light and fluffy marshmallow filling. Pure indulgence. Ideally, you will need an electric food mixer to make the marshmallow, although you could use an electric whisk.

Makes 12 Whoopie Pies

125g/4¼oz/8½ tbsp unsalted butter, softened
90g/3½oz/scant ½ cup soft light brown sugar
90g/3½oz/½ cup caster (superfine) sugar
1 egg
seeds of 1 vanilla pod (bean)
300g/11oz/2¾ cups plain (all-purpose) flour
50g/2oz cocoa powder
7.5ml/1½ tsp bicarbonate of soda (baking soda)
5ml/1 tsp salt
250ml/8fl oz/1 cup buttermilk
For the marshmallow filling
50ml/2fl oz/¼ cup boiling water
15ml/1 tbsp powdered gelatine
175g/6oz/generous ¾ cup caster (superfine) sugar
75ml/2½fl oz/⅓ cup golden (light corn) syrup
25ml/1½ tbsp cold water

1 Preheat the oven to 180°C/350°F/Gas 4. Line two baking trays with baking parchment or silicone mats.

2 For the cakes, place the butter and sugars in a bowl and beat together until light and creamy. Beat in the egg, then stir in the vanilla seeds until fully incorporated.

3 In a separate bowl, sift the flour with the cocoa powder, bicarbonate of soda and salt. Fold half of the dry ingredients into the butter mixture. Mix in the milk, then mix in the remainder of the dry ingredients.

4 Using a piping (pastry) bag fitted with a large plain nozzle, pipe 12 5cm/2in rounds of cake mixture 5cm/2in apart on each baking tray. Bake for 8–10 minutes, or until the cakes bounce back when gently pressed. Transfer to a wire rack to cool.

5 For the filling, put the boiling water in the bowl of an electric mixer and sprinkle with the gelatine. Whisk on low speed until the gelatine dissolves. In a pan, heat the sugar, golden syrup and cold water, stirring, until the mixture comes to a rolling boil. With the mixer on low, gradually add the hot syrup. Turn the mixer to high and whisk for 5 minutes, until the mixture turns very thick, pale and fluffy.

6 Using an oiled spoon, drop a large dollop of marshmallow on to the flat side of one cake, then top with the flat side of another and gently squeeze them together. Repeat to make 12 pies.

Energy 327kcal/1384kJ; Protein 5g; Carbohydrate 57g, of which sugars 37g; Fat 11g, of which saturates 7g; Cholesterol 45mg; Calcium 78mg; Fibre 0.9g; Sodium 379mg.

Mint Chocolate Chip Whoopie Pies

A chocolate lover's delight, these dense and complex whoopie pies are interspersed with luxurious dark chocolate chips and sandwiched together with a sinful but light chocolate buttercream. Try decorating the pies with chocolate shavings instead of cocoa powder.

Makes 24 Whoopie Pies

125g/4¼ oz/8½ tbsp unsalted butter, softened
175g/6oz/¾ cup light brown sugar
seeds of 1 vanilla pod (bean)
1 egg
325g/11½oz/scant 3 cups plain (all-purpose) flour
7.5ml/1½ tsp bicarbonate of soda (baking soda)
5ml/1 tsp salt
100g/3¾oz dark (bittersweet) chocolate, chopped into chunks
250ml/8fl oz/1 cup buttermilk

For the buttercream filling

300g/11oz/2¾ cups icing (confectioners') sugar
seeds of 1 vanilla pod (bean)
150g/5oz/10 tbsp unsalted butter, softened
90ml/6 tbsp double (heavy) cream
50g/2oz cocoa powder, plus extra for dusting
40g/1½oz plain (semisweet) chocolate chips

1　Preheat the oven to 180°C/350°F/Gas 4. Line two baking trays with baking parchment or silicone mats.

2　For the cakes, beat the butter, sugar and vanilla seeds until creamy. Beat in the egg. In a separate bowl, sift the flour with the bicarbonate of soda and salt, then stir in the chocolate. Fold half of the flour mixture into the butter mixture. Mix in the buttermilk, then the rest of the flour mixture.

3　Using a piping (pastry) bag fitted with a large plain nozzle, pipe 24 3cm/1¼in rounds of cake mixture (batter) 4cm/1½in apart on each of the baking trays. Bake for 10–12 minutes, or until the cakes bounce back when gently pressed. Transfer to a wire rack to cool.

4　For the filling, place the icing sugar, vanilla seeds and butter in a bowl. Using an electric whisk on medium speed, whisk until crumbly. Slowly whisk in the cream, then increase the speed to high and whisk until creamy and smooth. Fold in the sifted cocoa powder and chocolate chips.

5　Using a piping bag fitted with a star-shaped nozzle, pipe some filling on to the flat side of one cake and top with the flat side of another. Repeat to make 24 pies. Dust with cocoa powder.

Energy 273kcal/1151kJ; Protein 3g; Carbohydrate 35g, of which sugars 24g; Fat 15g, of which saturates 9g; Cholesterol 42mg; Calcium 48mg; Fibre 0.5g; Sodium 217mg.

Red Velvet Whoopie Pies

Red velvet is a classic American cake, deep red in colour, which forms the basis of these show-stopping whoopie pies. Gel food colouring works better than other food colouring types and only a teaspoonful is needed to achieve the desired deep red effect.

Makes 12 Whoopie Pies

125g/4¼oz/8½ tbsp unsalted butter, softened

175g/6oz/¾ cup light brown sugar

seeds of 1 vanilla pod (bean)

1 egg

300g/11oz/2¾ cups plain (all-purpose) flour

50g/2oz unsweetened cocoa powder

7.5ml/1½ tsp bicarbonate of soda (baking soda)

5ml/1 tsp salt

250ml/8fl oz/1 cup buttermilk

5ml/1 tsp red food colouring

For the marshmallow filling

50ml/2fl oz/¼ cup boiling water

15ml/1 tbsp powdered gelatine

175g/6oz/generous ¾ cup caster (superfine) sugar

75ml/2½fl oz/⅓ cup golden (light corn) syrup

25ml/1½ tbsp cold water

1 Preheat the oven to 180°C/350°F/Gas 4. Line two baking trays with baking parchment or silicone mats.

2 For the cakes, beat the butter, sugar and vanilla seeds until creamy. Beat in the egg.

3 In a separate bowl, sift the flour with the cocoa powder, bicarbonate of soda and salt. In a measuring jug (cup), mix the buttermilk and food colouring. Fold half of the dry ingredients into the butter mixture. Mix in the buttermilk mixture, then the rest of the dry ingredients. Using a piping (pastry) bag fitted with a large plain nozzle, pipe 12 5cm/2in rounds of mixture (batter) 5cm/2in apart on each baking tray.

4 Bake for 12–15 minutes, or until the cakes bounce back when gently pressed. Transfer to a wire rack to cool.

5 For the filling, put the boiling water in the bowl of an electric mixer and sprinkle with the gelatine. Whisk on low speed until the gelatine dissolves. In a pan, heat the sugar, golden syrup and cold water, stirring, until the mixture comes to a rolling boil. With the mixer on low, gradually add the hot syrup. Turn the mixer to high and whisk for 5 minutes, until the mixture turns very thick, pale and fluffy.

6 Using an oiled tablespoon, place a tablespoonful of the marshmallow on to the flat side of one cake and top with the flat side of another. Repeat to make 12 whoopie pies.

Energy 325kcal/1376kJ; Protein 5g; Carbohydrate 57g, of which sugars 37g; Fat 10g, of which saturates 6g; Cholesterol 44mg; Calcium 78mg; Fibre 0.9g; Sodium 382mg.

White Vanilla Whoopie Pies

Sandwiched together with a cream cheese filling and covered in melted white chocolate, these whoopie pies combine a light filling with deep and rich vanilla-flavoured cakes. Try adding a little raspberry jam in the middle with the filling for a splash of colour.

Makes 12 Whoopie Pies

130g/4½oz/generous ½ cup unsalted butter, softened
150g/5oz/¾ cup caster (superfine) sugar
seeds of 2 vanilla pods (beans)
1 egg
325g/11½oz/scant 3 cups plain (all-purpose) flour
7.5ml/1½ tsp bicarbonate of soda (baking soda)
5ml/1 tsp salt
50ml/2fl oz/¼ cup milk
150ml/¼ pint/⅔ cup buttermilk

For the cream cheese filling and chocolate topping

100ml/3½fl oz/scant ½ cup double (heavy) cream
150g/5oz/⅔ cup cream cheese
40g/1½oz/3 tbsp caster (superfine) sugar
seeds of 1 vanilla pod (bean)
150g/5oz white chocolate, melted

1 Preheat the oven to 180°C/350°F/Gas 4. Line two baking trays with baking parchment or silicone mats..

2 For the cakes, whisk the butter, sugar and vanilla seeds until light and fluffy. Whisk in the egg. In a separate bowl, sift the flour with the bicarbonate of soda and salt. Fold half of the dry ingredients into the butter mixture. Mix in the milk and buttermilk, then mix in the rest of the dry ingredients.

3 Using a piping (pastry) bag fitted with a large plain nozzle, pipe 12 5cm/2in rounds of cake mixture (batter) 5cm/2in apart on each baking tray. Bake for 12–15 minutes, or until the cakes bounce back when pressed. Transfer to a wire rack to cool.

4 For the filling, whip the cream until firm peaks form, then whisk in the cream cheese, sugar and vanilla seeds.

5 Using a piping bag fitted with a star-shaped nozzle, pipe a thick round of cream cheese filling on to the flat side of one cake and top with the flat side of another cake. Repeat with the remaining cakes and cream cheese filling to make 12 pies. Spread a little melted chocolate over the top of each pie. Allow the chocolate to set before serving.

Energy 512kcal/2152kJ; Protein 9g; Carbohydrate 67g, of which sugars 26g; Fat 25g, of which saturates 15g; Cholesterol 87mg; Calcium 155mg; Fibre 2.0g; Sodium 380mg.

Gluten-free Whoopie Pies

Dark and rich, these gluten-free chocolate whoopie pie cakes are delicious on their own, straight out of the oven, or equally yummy served cold, sandwiched together with chocolate buttercream. Adding xanthan gum to the cake batter will give a softer texture to the cakes.

Makes 12 Whoopie Pies

140g/4¾oz/9 tbsp unsalted butter, softened
165g/5½oz light brown sugar
seeds of 1 vanilla pod (bean)
2 eggs
200g/7oz gluten-free flour
50g/2oz/½ cup unsweetened cocoa powder
7.5ml/1½ tsp xanthan gum
5ml/1 tsp bicarbonate of soda (baking soda)
5ml/1 tsp salt
275ml/8½fl oz/generous 1 cup buttermilk
175ml/6fl oz/¾ cup milk

For the chocolate buttercream filling
200ml/7fl oz/scant 1 cup double (heavy) cream
45g/3 tbsp caster (superfine) sugar
25g/1oz unsweetened cocoa powder

1 Preheat the oven to 180°C/350°F/Gas 4. Line two baking trays with baking parchment or silicone mats.

2 For the cakes, whisk the butter, sugar and vanilla seeds until light and fluffy. Whisk in the eggs.

3 In a separate bowl, sift the flour with the cocoa powder, xanthan gum, bicarbonate of soda and salt. Fold half of the dry ingredients into the butter mixture. Mix in the buttermilk and milk, then add the remainder of the dry ingredients and mix until fully incorporated.

4 Using a piping (pastry) bag fitted with a large plain nozzle, pipe 12 5cm/2in rounds of cake mixture (batter) 5cm/2in apart on each baking tray. Bake for 12–15 minutes, or until the cakes bounce back when pressed. Transfer to a wire rack to cool.

5 For the filling, whisk the cream and sugar in a bowl with an electric whisk on high until just stiff. Gently fold in the sifted cocoa powder.

6 Using a piping bag fitted with a star-shaped nozzle, pipe some filling on to the flat side of one cake and top with the flat side of another. Repeat to make 12 pies.

Energy 326kcal/1387kJ; Protein 4g; Carbohydrate 34g, of which sugars 20g; Fat 21g, of which saturates 13g; Cholesterol 89mg; Calcium 62mg; Fibre 0.9g; Sodium 152mg.

Mocha Whoopie Pies

For caffeine lovers, these whoopie pies deliver a real coffee kick. Topped and filled with a light and sweet buttercream filling, they are best served with a tall glass of cold milk. Some of the luxurious filling is reserved for the top, so they look beautifully elegant

Makes 12 Whoopie Pies

130g/4½oz/generous ½ cup
  unsalted butter, softened
150g/5oz/¾ cup caster (superfine)
  sugar
seeds of 1 vanilla pod (bean)
1 egg
325g/11½oz/scant 3 cups plain
  (all-purpose) flour
7.5ml/1½ tsp bicarbonate of soda
  (baking soda)
5ml/1 tsp salt
150ml/5fl oz/⅔ cup buttermilk
50ml/2fl oz/¼ cup milk
60ml/4 tbsp coffee dissolved in
  15ml/1 tbsp hot water

**For the buttercream filling and
  topping**

2 egg whites
125g/4½oz/generous ½ cup
  caster (superfine) sugar
225g/8oz/1 cup unsalted
  butter, softened
30ml/2 tbsp coffee, dissolved in
  7.5ml/1½ tsp hot water
40g/1½oz dark (bittersweet)
  chocolate

1 Preheat the oven to 180°C/350°F/Gas 4. Line two baking trays with baking parchment or silicone mats.

2 For the cakes, whisk the butter, sugar and vanilla seeds together until light and fluffy. Whisk in the egg. In a separate bowl, sift the flour with the bicarbonate of soda and salt. In a measuring jug (cup), mix the buttermilk, milk and dissolved coffee.

3 Fold half of the dry ingredients into the butter mixture. Mix in the buttermilk mixture, then add the remainder of the dry ingredients and mix well. Using a piping (pastry) bag fitted with a large plain nozzle, pipe 12 5cm/2in rounds of cake mixture (batter) 5cm/2in apart on each baking tray. Bake for 12–15 minutes, or until the cakes bounce back when pressed. Transfer to a wire rack to cool.

4 For the filling, put the egg whites and sugar in a heatproof bowl set over a pan of simmering water. Using an electric whisk, whisk until the sugar has dissolved and the mixture turns white and is hot. Remove from the heat and continue to whisk on high speed until the bowl starts to cool down. Turn the speed to low and whisk in the butter, a little at a time. Gently fold in the dissolved coffee.

5 Using a piping (pastry) bag fitted with a star-shaped nozzle, pipe some of the filling on to the flat side of one cake and top with the flat side of another. Repeat to make 12 pies. Pipe the remaining filling on the tops of the pies, then grate chocolate over the top.

Energy 439kcal/1850kJ; Protein 5g; Carbohydrate 48g, of which sugars 27g; Fat 26g, of which saturates 17g; Cholesterol 88mg; Calcium 73mg; Fibre 1.0g; Sodium 335mg.

Banana Bread Whoopie Pies

Comforting and sweet, these whoopies are excellent served while still warm, straight from the oven. Filled with walnut buttercream, they are moist and luxurious with a hint of cinnamon, and can also be toasted just before assembling.

Makes 12 Whoopie Pies

150g/5oz/10 tbsp unsalted butter, softened
150g/5oz/generous ½ cup light brown sugar
seeds of 1 vanilla pod (bean)
2 eggs
325g/11½oz/scant 3 cups plain (all-purpose) flour
7.5ml/1½ tsp bicarbonate of soda (baking soda)
5ml/1 tsp ground cinnamon
2.5ml/½ tsp salt
100ml/3½fl oz/scant ½ cup buttermilk
200g/7oz mashed bananas

For the buttercream filling
300g/11oz/2¾ cups icing (confectioners') sugar, plus extra for dusting
seeds of 1 vanilla pod (bean)
150g/5oz/10 tbsp unsalted butter, softened
50ml/2fl oz/¼ cup double (heavy) cream
75g/3oz/¾ cup walnuts, chopped

1 Preheat the oven to 180°C/350°F/Gas 4. Line two baking trays with baking parchment or silicone mats.

2 For the cakes, cream the butter, sugar and vanilla seeds until light and fluffy. Beat in the eggs, one at a time. In a separate bowl, sift the flour with the bicarbonate of soda, cinnamon and salt. Fold half of the dry ingredients into the butter mixture. Mix in the buttermilk, then the remainder of the dry ingredients. Fold in the bananas.

3 Using a piping (pastry) bag fitted with a large plain nozzle, pipe 12 5cm/2in rounds of cake mixture (batter) 5cm/2in apart on each baking tray. Bake for 12–15 minutes, or until the cakes bounce back when gently pressed. Transfer to a wire rack to cool.

4 For the filling, place the icing sugar, vanilla seeds and butter in a bowl. Using an electric whisk on medium speed, whisk until crumbly. Slowly whisk in the cream, then increase the speed to high and whisk until smooth. Fold in the walnuts.

5 Using a piping bag fitted with a large plain nozzle, pipe small blobs of the filling on to the flat side of one cake, then top with the flat side of another. Repeat to make 12 pies. Dust with icing sugar, using a doily to create a pattern.

Energy 520kcal/2191kJ; Protein 5g; Carbohydrate 64g, of which sugars 43g; Fat 29g, of which saturates 16g; Cholesterol 102mg; Calcium 77mg; Fibre 1.9g; Sodium 250mg.

Oatmeal and Dried-fruit Whoopie Pies

These hearty whoopie pies, filled with wholesome oats and juicy raisins and sultanas, are a perfect mid-morning treat. They are flavoured with a hint of cinnamon and sandwiched together with a creamy cheese filling, and go well with a cup of tea or coffee.

Makes 12 Whoopie Pies

130g/4½oz/generous ½ cup unsalted butter, softened
150g/5oz/¾ cup caster (superfine) sugar
seeds of 1 vanilla pod (bean)
1 egg
325g/11½oz/scant 3 cups plain (all-purpose) flour
7.5ml/1½ tsp bicarbonate of soda (baking soda)
5ml/1 tsp ground cinnamon
5ml/1 tsp salt
150ml/5 fl oz/⅔ cup buttermilk
50ml/2fl oz/¼ cup milk
40g/1½oz/½ cup rolled oats
100g/3¾oz/⅔ cup mixed raisins and sultanas (golden raisins)

For the mascarpone filling
120ml/4fl oz/½ cup double (heavy) cream
125g/4½oz/generous ½ cup mascarpone
25g/1oz/2 tbsp caster (superfine) sugar
seeds from 1 vanilla pod (bean)

1 Preheat the oven to 180°C/350°F/Gas 4. Line two baking trays with baking parchment or silicone mats.

2 For the cakes, whisk the butter, sugar and vanilla seeds in a bowl until light and fluffy. Whisk in the egg.

3 In a separate bowl, sift the flour with the bicarbonate of soda, cinnamon and salt. Fold half of the dry ingredients into the butter mixture. Add the buttermilk and milk, and mix well. Mix in the remaining dry ingredients, then stir in the oats, raisins and sultanas.

4 Using a piping (pastry) bag fitted with a large plain nozzle, pipe 12 5cm/2in rounds of cake mixture (batter) 5cm/2in apart on each baking tray. Bake for 12–15 minutes, or until the cakes bounce back when pressed. Transfer to a wire rack to cool.

5 For the filling, whip the cream until medium-firm peaks form, then whisk in the mascarpone, sugar and vanilla seeds until stiff peaks form. Using a piping bag fitted with a small star-shaped nozzle, pipe some filling on to the flat side of one cake and top with the flat side of another. Repeat to make 12 pies.

Energy 366kcal/1537kJ; Protein 5g; Carbohydrate 44g, of which sugars 21g; Fat 20g, of which saturates 13g; Cholesterol 70mg; Calcium 88mg; Fibre 1.7g; Sodium 334mg.

Orange Polenta Whoopie Pies

These dense and substantial whoopie pies combine the zesty flavours of orange and chocolate in a delicious creamy filling that sandwiches together soft polenta cakes. You can try experimenting with the rind and juice of other citrus fruits, such as mandarins or limes.

Makes 12 Whoopie Pies

175g/6oz/1½ cups instant polenta

juice of 1 orange

125g/4¼ oz/8½ tbsp unsalted butter, softened

200g/7oz/scant 1 cup soft light brown sugar

2 eggs

450g/1lb/4 cups plain (all-purpose) flour

7.5ml/1½ tsp bicarbonate of soda (baking soda)

5ml/1 tsp salt

250ml/8fl oz/1 cup buttermilk

For the cream filling and chocolate topping

250ml/8fl oz/1 cup double (heavy) cream

25g/1oz/2 tbsp caster (superfine) sugar

grated rind and juice of ½ orange

20g/¾ oz unsweetened cocoa powder

100g/3¾ oz dark (bittersweet) chocolate, melted

1 Preheat the oven to 180°C/350°F/Gas 4. Line two baking trays with baking parchment or silicone mats. Place the polenta in a bowl and stir in the orange juice. Set aside to soak.

2 For the cakes, place the butter and brown sugar in a bowl and whisk together until light and creamy. Whisk in the eggs, one at a time. In a separate bowl, sift the flour with the bicarbonate of soda and salt. Add the dry ingredients to the butter mixture in three batches, alternating with the buttermilk. Fold in the polenta.

3 Using a piping (pastry) bag fitted with a large plain nozzle, pipe 12 5cm/2in rounds of cake mixture (batter) about 5cm/2in apart on each baking tray. Bake for 12–15 minutes, or until the cakes bounce back when gently pressed. Transfer to a wire rack to cool.

4 To make the filling, whip the cream until stiff peaks form. Add the sugar, orange rind and juice and cocoa powder, and whisk until thick.

5 Using a piping bag fitted with a star-shaped nozzle, pipe some of the filling on to the flat side of one cake and top with the flat side of another. Repeat to make 12 pies. Drizzle over the melted chocolate.

Energy 432kcal/1815kJ; Protein 7g; Carbohydrate 57g, of which sugars 23g; Fat 21g, of which saturates 13g; Cholesterol 79mg; Calcium 95mg; Fibre 1.7g; Sodium 305mg.

Raspberry Swirl Whoopie Pies

Pretty and pink, these raspberry swirl whoopies are eye-catching and can be made at any time of the year with frozen raspberries. If you want to make a topping, simply mash some raspberries with some icing (confectioners') sugar and drizzle on top.

Makes 12 Whoopie Pies

125g/4¼oz/8½ tbsp unsalted butter, softened
175g/6oz/¾ cup soft light brown sugar
seeds of 1 vanilla pod (bean)
1 egg
350g/12oz/3 cups plain (all-purpose) flour
7.5ml/1½ tsp bicarbonate of soda (baking soda)
5ml/1 tsp salt
250ml/8fl oz/1 cup buttermilk
5ml/1 tsp red food colouring

For the filling

200ml/7fl oz/scant 1 cup whipping cream
150g/5oz/scant 1 cup fresh raspberries

1 Preheat the oven to 180°C/350°F/Gas 4. Line two baking trays with baking parchment or silicone mats.

2 For the cakes, place the butter, brown sugar and vanilla seeds in a bowl and whisk together until light and creamy. Add the egg and whisk until fully incorporated.

3 In a separate bowl, sift the flour with the bicarbonate of soda and salt. Fold half of the dry ingredients into the butter mixture. Mix in the buttermilk, then add the rest of the dry ingredients and mix until fully incorporated. Transfer half of the cake mixture (batter) into another bowl and fold the red food colouring into this cake mixture.

4 Using a piping (pastry) bag fitted with a large plain nozzle, pipe 12 3cm/1¼in rounds of vanilla cake mixture 5cm/2in apart on each baking tray. Place a dollop of the red mixture on each round and, using the tip of a knife, swirl a figure of eight to create a marbled effect.

5 Bake for 12–15 minutes, or until the cakes bounce back when pressed. Transfer to a wire rack to cool.

6 For the filling, whip the cream in a bowl until stiff peaks form. Squash the raspberries with the back of a fork, then fold them into the cream.

7 Place a tablespoonful of raspberry cream filling on to the flat side of one cake and top with the flat side of another. Repeat to make 12 pies.

Energy 312kcal/1313kJ; Protein 5g; Carbohydrate 40g, of which sugars 17g; Fat 16g, of which saturates 10g; Cholesterol 61mg; Calcium 91mg; Fibre 1.9g; Sodium 331mg.

Strawberry Lime Cheesecake Whoopie Pies

The classic flavours of strawberry cheesecake are always a delight, and they are even better in a whoopie pie. These whoopies are filled with a creamy ricotta cheese mixture containing chopped strawberries, and are perfect for the summer when the berries are at their best.

Makes 12 Whoopie Pies

125g/4¼oz/8½ tbsp unsalted butter, softened
175g/6oz/¾ cup soft light brown sugar
seeds of 1 vanilla pod (bean)
1 egg
350g/12oz/3 cups plain (all-purpose) flour
7.5ml/1½ tsp bicarbonate of soda (baking powder)
5ml/1 tsp salt
finely grated rind of 2 limes
250ml/8fl oz/1 cup buttermilk
For the strawberry cheese filling
100ml/3½fl oz/scant ½ cup double (heavy) cream
100g/3¼oz/½ cup ricotta cheese
25g/1oz/2 caster (superfine) sugar
seeds of 1 vanilla pod (bean)
75g/3oz/¾ cup fresh strawberries
For the topping
100g/3¼oz white chocolate, melted
red and pink sprinkles

1 Preheat the oven to 180°C/350°F/Gas 4. Line two baking trays with baking parchment or silicone mats.

2 For the cakes, whisk the butter, sugar and vanilla seeds in a bowl until light and creamy. Add the egg and whisk until fully incorporated.

3 In a separate bowl, sift the flour with the bicarbonate of soda and salt and then add the lime rind. Fold half of the dry ingredients into the butter mixture. Mix in the buttermilk, then the remainder of the dry ingredients.

4 Using a piping (pastry) bag fitted with a large plain nozzle, pipe 12 3cm/1¼in rounds of cake mixture (batter) 5cm/2in apart on each baking tray. Bake for 12–15 minutes, or until the cakes bounce back when pressed. Transfer to a wire rack to cool.

5 For the filling, whip the cream in a bowl until stiff peaks form, then whisk in the ricotta cheese, sugar and vanilla seeds, mixing well. Hull and chop the strawberries, then fold them into the mixture.

6 Place a heaped tablespoonful of filling on to the flat side of one cake and top with the flat side of another. Repeat to make 12 pies. Spread a little melted chocolate over the top of each pie, and decorate with sprinkles.

Energy 356kcal/1501kJ; Protein 6g; Carbohydrate 47g, of which sugars 25g; Fat 18g, of which saturates 11g; Cholesterol 60mg; Calcium 128mg; Fibre 1.2g; Sodium 347mg.

Walnut Chocolate Crunch Whoopie Pies

These whoopie pies are deliciously moist, moreish and crunchy with a rich chocolate base. They make the perfect combination for chocoholics and nut fanatics alike. To finish them off perfectly they are drizzled decadently with dulce de leche.

Makes 12 Whoopie Pies

130g/4½oz/generous ½ cup unsalted butter, softened
150g/5oz/¾ cup caster (superfine) sugar
seeds of 1 vanilla pod (bean)
1 egg
300g/11oz/2¾ cups plain (all-purpose) flour
40g/1½oz unsweetened cocoa powder
7.5ml/1½ tsp bicarbonate of soda (baking soda)
5ml/1 tsp salt
50ml/2fl oz/¼ cup milk
150ml/5fl oz/⅔ cup buttermilk
100g/3¾oz/scant 1 cup walnuts, chopped

For the filling

250ml/8fl oz/1 cup double (heavy) cream
45ml/3 tbsp dulce de leche

For the topping

175ml/6fl oz/¾ cup dulce de leche
12 walnut halves

1 Preheat the oven to 180°C/350°F/Gas 4. Line two baking trays with baking parchment or silicone mats.

2 For the cakes, whisk the butter, sugar and vanilla seeds together until light and creamy. Whisk in the egg. In a separate bowl, sift the flour with the cocoa powder, bicarbonate of soda and salt.

3 Fold half of the dry ingredients into the butter mixture. Mix in the milk and buttermilk, then the rest of the dry ingredients. Fold in the walnuts.

4 Using a piping (pastry) bag fitted with a large plain nozzle, pipe 12 5cm/2in rounds of cake mixture (batter) 5cm/2in apart on each baking tray. Bake for 12–15 minutes, or until the cakes bounce back when pressed. Transfer to a wire rack to cool.

5 For the filling, whip the cream until stiff peaks form. Whisk in the dulce de leche. Using a piping bag fitted with a star-shaped nozzle, pipe some filling on to the flat side of one cake and top with the flat side of another. Repeat to make 12 pies. Drizzle a tablespoon of dulce de leche over the top of each pie and decorate with a walnut half.

Energy 545kcal/2285kJ; Protein 9g; Carbohydrate 55g, of which sugars 35g; Fat 34g, of which saturates 16g; Cholesterol 86mg; Calcium 193mg; Fibre 1.6g; Sodium 408mg.

Cola Cake Whoopie Pies

The fizzy cola drink in these whoopie pie cakes gives a lovely lightness to the pies, and the vanilla intensifies the sweet cola flavour. If you want to achieve a deeper cola flavour, try adding a few drops of cola extract to the cake mixture.

Makes 12 Whoopie Pies

130g/4½oz/generous ½ cup
  unsalted butter, softened
150g/5oz/¾ cup caster
  (superfine) sugar
1 egg
325g/11½oz/scant 3 cups plain
  (all-purpose) flour
7.5ml/1½ tsp bicarbonate of soda
  (baking soda)
5ml/1 tsp salt
150ml/5fl oz/⅔ cup cola drink

For the filling and icing

300g/11oz/2¾ cups icing
  (confectioners') sugar
seeds of 1 vanilla pod (bean)
150g/5oz/10 tbsp unsalted
  butter, softened
90ml/6 tbsp double (heavy) cream
50g/2oz cola-flavoured hard-
  boiled sweets (candies), crushed

For the topping

150g/5oz/1¼ cups icing
  (confectioners') sugar
25ml/1½ tbsp cola drink
cola bottle sweets, to decorate

1 Preheat the oven to 180°C/350°F/Gas 4. Line two baking trays with baking parchment or silicone mats.

2 For the cakes, beat the butter and sugar until light and creamy. Beat in the egg. In a separate bowl, sift the flour with the bicarbonate of soda and salt. Fold half of the dry ingredients into the butter mixture.

3 Mix in the cola, then mix in the remainder of the dry ingredients.

4 Using a piping (pastry) bag fitted with a large plain nozzle, pipe 12 5cm/2in rounds of cake mixture (batter) 5cm/2in apart on each baking tray. Bake for 12–15 minutes, or until the cakes bounce back when gently pressed. Transfer to a wire rack to cool.

5 For the filling, place the icing sugar, vanilla seeds and butter in a bowl. Using an electric whisk on medium speed, whisk together until lightly crumbly. Slowly whisk in the cream, then increase the speed to high and whisk until the mixture is smooth.

6 Using a piping bag fitted with a tiny nozzle, pipe a thin line of filling around the edge of each cake. Roll in crushed cola sweets.

7 Using a small plain nozzle, pipe some filling on to the flat side of one cake and top with the flat side of another. Repeat to make 12 pies.

8 For the icing, mix the icing sugar and cola drink together to form a smooth paste. Spread a little icing over the tops of the pies and top off with cola bottles.

Energy 529kcal/2237kJ; Protein 3g; Carbohydrate 79g, of which sugars 56g; Fat 24g, of which saturates 15g; Cholesterol 84mg; Calcium 51mg; Fibre 1.0g; Sodium 321mg.

Mini Jam Doughnut Whoopie Pies

Made to resemble jam doughnuts, these mini whoopie pies are innovative and fun. They hide their strawberry jam surprise inside the cakes, just like a real jam doughnut. Try using different jams such as peach, apricot or raspberry. A real winner, whatever the jam.

Makes 24 Whoopie Pies

150g/5oz/10 tbsp unsalted butter, softened
150g/5oz/generous ½ cup soft light brown sugar
50g/2oz/¼ cup caster (superfine) sugar
seeds of 1 vanilla pod (bean)
2 eggs
350g/12oz/3 cups plain (all-purpose) flour
7.5ml/1½ tsp bicarbonate of soda (baking soda)
5ml/1 tsp salt
150ml/5fl oz/⅔ cup buttermilk

For the filling
300g/11oz/generous 1 cup strawberry jam

For the topping
150g/5oz/1¼ cups icing (confectioners') sugar
25ml/1½ tbsp cold water
25g/1oz/2 tbsp granulated (white) sugar, for sprinkling

1 Preheat the oven to 180°C/350°F/Gas 4. Line two baking trays with baking parchment or silicone mats. Whisk the butter, sugars and vanilla seeds together until light and creamy. Whisk in the eggs, one at a time.

2 In a separate bowl, sift the flour with the bicarbonate of soda and salt. Fold half of the dry ingredients into the butter mixture. Mix in the buttermilk, then the rest of the dry ingredients.

3 Using a piping (pastry) bag fitted with a large plain nozzle, pipe 24 3cm/ 1¼in rounds of cake mixture (batter) 4cm/1½in apart on each baking tray. Bake for 10–12 minutes, until golden. Transfer to a wire rack to cool.

4 Scoop out about a teaspoon of cake from the flat side of two cakes. Fill the holes with jam and sandwich them together. Repeat to make 24 pies.

5 Meanwhile, mix the icing sugar and water together to make a smooth icing. Spread a little icing over the top of each pie and sprinkle with sugar.

Energy 191kcal/809kJ; Protein 3g; Carbohydrate 37g, of which sugars 26g; Fat 5g, of which saturates 3g; Cholesterol 32mg; Calcium 37mg; Fibre 0.7g; Sodium 169mg.

Runny Honey Whoopie Pies

Fragrant but not overly sweet, these whoopie pies will be a favourite for honey lovers everywhere. The honey buttercream filling is delicate and sumptuous at the same time, but you could always substitute any of the other fillings in this book, if you like.

Makes 12 Whoopie Pies

125g/4¼ oz/8½ tbsp unsalted
   butter, softened
175g/6oz/¾ cup light brown
   sugar
seeds of 1 vanilla pod (bean)
1 egg
350g/12oz/3 cups plain
   (all-purpose) flour
7.5ml/1½ tsp bicarbonate of
   soda (baking soda)
5ml/1 tsp salt
250ml/8fl oz/1 cup buttermilk
30ml/2 tbsp clear honey

For the buttercream filling and
   topping
300g/11oz/2¾ cups icing
   (confectioners') sugar
seeds of 1 vanilla pod (bean)
165g/5½oz/scant ¾ cup unsalted
   butter, softened
90ml/6 tbsp double (heavy)
   cream
105ml/7 tbsp clear honey, plus
   extra for drizzling

1   Preheat the oven to 180°C/350°F/Gas 4. Line two baking trays with baking parchment or silicone mats.

2   For the cakes, whisk the butter, sugar and vanilla seeds together until light and creamy. Whisk in the egg. In a separate bowl, sift the flour with the bicarbonate of soda and salt. Fold half of the dry ingredients into the butter mixture. Mix in the buttermilk, then the rest of the dry ingredients. Fold in the honey, mixing well.

3   Using a piping (pastry) bag fitted with a large plain nozzle, pipe 12 5cm/2in rounds of cake mixture (batter) 5cm/2in apart on each of the baking trays. Bake for 12–15 minutes and allow to cool.

4   To make the filling, place the icing sugar, vanilla seeds and butter in a bowl. Using an electric whisk on medium speed, whisk the ingredients together until lightly crumbly. Slowly whisk in the cream, then increase the speed to high and whisk until the mixture is creamy and smooth.

5   Mix in the honey. Pipe some filling on to the flat side of one cake and top with the flat side of another. Repeat to make 12 pies. Drizzle a little honey over each pie.

Energy 529kcal/2234kJ; Protein 5g; Carbohydrate 75g, of which sugars 53g; Fat 25g, of which saturates 16g; Cholesterol 87mg; Calcium 111mg; Fibre 1.1g; Sodium 369mg.

Tiramisu whoopie pies

This take on the Italian classic can be made in advance as the flavours will improve as they infuse. Wrap the pies in clear film (plastic wrap) and refrigerate for up to 2 days. When ready to serve, bring them back to room temperature and dust with cocoa powder.

Makes 12 Whoopie Pies

125g/4¼oz/8½ tbsp unsalted butter, softened

175g/6oz/¾ cup light brown sugar

seeds of 1 vanilla pod (bean)

1 egg

350g/12oz/3 cups plain (all-purpose) flour

7.5ml/1½ tsp bicarbonate of soda (baking soda)

5ml/1 tsp salt

250ml/8fl oz/1 cup buttermilk

60ml/4 tbsp coffee dissolved in 15ml/1 tbsp hot water

For the mascarpone filling

250ml/8fl oz/1 cup double (heavy) cream

200g/7oz/scant 1 cup mascarpone

65g/2½oz/5 tbsp caster (superfine) sugar

50ml/2fl oz/¼ cup Marsala (optional)

unsweetened cocoa powder, for dusting

1 Preheat the oven to 180°C/350°F/Gas 4. Line two baking trays with baking parchment or silicone mats.

2 For the cakes, place the butter in a bowl with the brown sugar and vanilla seeds and whisk together until light and fluffy. Whisk in the egg.

3 In a separate bowl, sift the flour with the bicarbonate of soda and salt. In a measuring jug (cup), mix together the buttermilk and dissolved coffee.

4 Fold half of the dry ingredients into the butter mixture. Mix in the buttermilk mixture, then the remainder of the dry ingredients.

5 Using a piping (pastry) bag fitted with a large plain nozzle, pipe 12 5cm/2in rounds of cake mixture (batter) 5cm/2in apart on each baking tray. Bake for 12–15 minutes, or until the cakes bounce back when pressed. Transfer to a wire rack to cool.

6 For the filling, whisk the cream, mascarpone, sugar and Marsala (if using) together until stiff peaks form.

7 Using a piping bag fitted with a star-shaped nozzle, pipe some filling on to the flat side of one cake and top with the flat side of another. Repeat to make 12 pies. Dust the top of each pie with cocoa powder.

Energy 446kcal/1870kJ; Protein 6g; Carbohydrate 46g, of which sugars 23g; Fat 28g, of which saturates 18g; Cholesterol 90mg; Calcium 107mg; Fibre 1.1 g; Sodium 342mg.

Chocolate Nut Whoopie Pies

Moist and nutty chocolate cakes are sandwiched together with a chocolate hazelnut filling, and topped with melted dark chocolate to create these indulgent whoopie pies. The cake mixture is quite chunky, so it is best to use an ice cream scoop to form the cake rounds.

Makes 12 Whoopie Pies

130g/4½oz/generous ½ cup
  unsalted butter, softened
150g/5oz/¾ cup caster
  (superfine) sugar
seeds of 1 vanilla pod (bean)
1 egg
300g/11oz/2¾ cups plain
  (all-purpose) flour
25g/1oz unsweetened cocoa
  powder
7.5ml/1½ tsp bicarbonate of
  soda (baking soda)
5ml/1 tsp salt
100g/3¾oz/scant 1 cup dry
  roasted unsalted peanuts,
  roughly chopped
150ml/5fl oz/⅔ cup buttermilk
50ml/2fl oz/¼ cup milk
For the filling and topping
300g/11oz chocolate hazelnut
  spread
100g/3¾oz dark (bittersweet)
  chocolate, melted
50g/2oz/½ cup chopped
  hazelnuts

1 Preheat the oven to 180°C/350°F/Gas 4. Line two baking trays with baking parchment or silicone mats.

2 For the cakes, whisk the butter, sugar and vanilla seeds together until light and creamy. Whisk in the egg. In a separate bowl, sift the flour with the cocoa powder, bicarbonate of soda and salt, then stir in the peanuts. Fold half of the flour mixture into the butter mixture. Mix in the buttermilk and milk, then the rest of the flour mixture.

3 Using an ice cream scoop or 2 tablespoons, scoop or spoon 12 5cm/2in rounds of cake mixture (batter) 5cm/2in apart on each of the baking trays. Bake for 12–15 minutes, or until the cakes bounce back when gently pressed. Transfer to a wire rack and leave to cool completely before assembling.

4 To assemble the pies, place about 2 tablespoonfuls of the chocolate hazelnut spread on the flat side of one cake and top with the flat side of another. Repeat with the remaining cakes and filling to make 12 pies.

5 Spoon a little melted chocolate on to the top of each pie, spreading the chocolate evenly. Lightly sprinkle each pie with chopped hazelnuts.

Energy 467kcal/1964kJ; Protein 6g; Carbohydrate 58g, of which sugars 39g; Fat 25g, of which saturates 8g; Cholesterol 46mg; Calcium 74mg; Fibre 1.3g; Sodium 357mg.

Pecan Whoopie Pies

The American classic pecan pie is given a makeover by taking the traditional flavours and using them to create a fluffy whoopie pie with rich, buttery pecan nuts. The simple whipped cream and maple syrup filling complements the pecans beautifully.

Makes 12 Whoopie Pies

125g/4¼oz/8½ tbsp unsalted butter, softened
175g/6oz/¾ cup light brown sugar
seeds of 1 vanilla pod (bean)
1 egg
350g/12oz/3 cups plain (all-purpose) flour
7.5ml/1½ tsp bicarbonate of soda (baking soda)
5ml/1 tsp salt
250ml/8fl oz/1 cup buttermilk
90g/3½oz/scant 1 cup pecan nuts, roughly chopped

For the filling
250ml/8fl oz/1 cup double (heavy) cream
45ml/3 tbsp maple syrup

For the topping
200g/7oz dulce de leche
12 pecan halves

1 Preheat the oven to 180°C/350°F/Gas 4. Line two baking trays with baking parchment or silicone mats.

2 For the cakes, whisk the butter, brown sugar and vanilla seeds together until light and creamy. Whisk in the egg. In a separate bowl, sift the flour with the bicarbonate of soda and salt. Fold half of the dry ingredients into the butter mixture. Mix in the buttermilk, then the remainder of the dry ingredients. Fold in the chopped pecans, mixing well.

3 Using an ice cream scoop or 2 tablespoons, scoop or spoon 12 5cm/2in rounds of cake mixture (batter) 5cm/2in apart on each of the baking trays. Bake for 12–15 minutes, or until the cakes bounce back when gently pressed. Transfer to a wire rack and leave to cool.

4 For the filling, whip the cream until stiff peaks form. Add the maple syrup and whisk to combine.

5 Place a tablespoonful of filling on to the flat side of one cake and top with the flat side of another. Repeat to make 12 pies. Evenly spread a tablespoonful of dulce de leche over the top of each pie and decorate each with a pecan half.

Energy 562kcal/2356kJ; Protein 9g; Carbohydrate 61g, of which sugars 38g; Fat 34g, of which saturates 16g; Cholesterol 84mg; Calcium 196mg; Fibre 1.1g; Sodium 37

Banoffee and Walnut Whoopie Pies

Banoffee pie is a classic flavour combination, ideal for the super sweet-toothed! Whipped cream for the filling balances the sweetness of the caramel. Another nutty cake mixture, you will probably find it easier to scoop or spoon the mixture on to baking trays than to pipe it.

Makes 12 Whoopie Pies

130g/4½oz/generous ½ cup
  unsalted butter, softened
150g/5oz/generous ½ cup light
  brown sugar
1 egg, beaten
300g/11oz/2¾ cups plain
  (all-purpose) flour
7.5ml/1½ tsp bicarbonate of
  soda (baking soda)
5ml/1 tsp salt
2.5ml/½ tsp ground cinnamon
a pinch of freshly grated nutmeg
50ml/2fl oz/¼ cup milk
150ml/5fl oz/⅔ cup buttermilk
200g/7oz mashed bananas
40g/1½oz/scant ½ cup walnuts,
  roughly chopped
For the filling
150ml/¼ pint/⅔ cup double
  (heavy) cream
100g/3¾oz dulce de leche

1 Preheat the oven to 180°C/350°F/Gas 4. Line two baking trays with baking parchment or silicone mats.

2 For the cakes, whisk the butter and brown sugar together until light and fluffy. Whisk in the egg. In a separate bowl, sift the flour with the bicarbonate of soda, salt, cinnamon and nutmeg. Fold half of the dry ingredients into the butter mixture. Mix in the milk and buttermilk, then the remainder of the dry ingredients.

3 Fold in the mashed bananas and walnuts, mixing well.

4 Using an ice cream scoop or two tablespoons, scoop or spoon 12 5cm/2in rounds of cake mixture (batter) 5cm/2in apart on each baking tray. Bake for 12–15 minutes, or until the cakes bounce back when gently pressed. Transfer to a wire rack to cool.

5 To make the filling, whip the cream until stiff peaks form. Fold in the dulce de leche.

6 Using a piping (pastry) bag fitted with a star-shaped nozzle, pipe some whipped cream filling on to the flat side of one cake and top with the flat side of another. Repeat to make 12 pies.

Energy 382kcal/1604kJ; Protein 6g; Carbohydrate 46g, of which sugars 27g; Fat 21g, of which saturates 12g; Cholesterol 68mg; Calcium 127mg; Fibre 1.6g; Sodium 349mg.

Chocolate Date Whoopie Pies

Sumptuous and rich, these unusual whoopie pies are for those with a really sweet tooth. Fluffy chocolate cakes with chunks of chewy dates are sandwiched together by a sticky dulce de leche filling, which oozes out when you take your first bite.

Makes 12 Whoopie Pies

125g/4¼oz/8½ tbsp unsalted butter, softened
175g/6oz/¾ cup light brown sugar
seeds of 1 vanilla pod (bean)
1 egg
300g/11oz/2¾ cups plain (all-purpose) flour
50g/2oz unsweetened cocoa powder
7.5ml/1½ tsp bicarbonate of soda (baking soda)
5ml/1 tsp salt
75g/3oz/½ cup dates, stoned (pitted) and chopped
250ml/8fl oz/1 cup buttermilk
For the filling and topping
200g/7oz dulce de leche
icing (confectioners') sugar, for dusting

1 Preheat the oven to 180°C/350°F/Gas 4. Line two baking trays with baking parchment or silicone mats.

2 For the cakes, whisk the butter, brown sugar and vanilla seeds until light and fluffy. Add the egg and whisk well.

3 In a separate bowl, sift the flour with the cocoa powder, bicarbonate of soda and salt, then stir in the dates.

4 Fold the flour mixture into the butter mixture in three stages, alternating each addition with the buttermilk, until all of the flour mixture and the buttermilk have been incorporated.

5 Using a piping (pastry) bag fitted with a large plain nozzle, pipe 12 5cm/2in rounds of cake mixture (batter) 5cm/2in apart on each baking tray. Bake for 12–15 minutes, or until the cakes bounce back when pressed. Transfer to a wire rack and leave to cool completely.

6 Spread a tablespoonful of dulce de leche on to the flat side of one cake and cover with the flat side of another. Repeat to make 12 pies. Dust with sifted icing sugar.

Energy 327kcal/1384kJ; Protein 5g; Carbohydrate 57g, of which sugars 37g; Fat 11g, of which saturates 7g; Cholesterol 45mg; Calcium 78mg; Fibre 0.9g; Sodium 379mg.

Mississippi Mud Whoopie Pies

These whoopie pies combine rich chocolate cakes with a filling of dark chocolate ice cream. They are based on the flavours of the classic American dessert, but contain a novel ice cream filling. Only fill them with ice cream when you are ready to serve them.

Makes 12 Whoopie Pies

125g/4¼oz/8½ tbsp unsalted butter, softened
175g/6oz/¾ cup light brown sugar
seeds of 1 vanilla pod (bean)
1 egg
300g/11oz/2¾ cups plain (all-purpose) flour
50g/2oz cocoa powder
7.5ml/1½ tsp bicarbonate of soda (baking soda)
5ml/1 tsp salt
250ml/8fl oz/1 cup buttermilk

For the filling and topping
400ml/14fl oz/1⅔ cups dark chocolate ice cream
150g/5oz dark (bittersweet) chocolate, melted
multicoloured sprinkles, to decorate

1 Preheat the oven to 180°C/350°F/Gas 4. Line two baking trays with baking parchment or silicone mats.

2 For the cakes, whisk the butter, brown sugar and vanilla seeds together until light and creamy. Whisk in the egg.

3 In a separate bowl, sift the flour with the cocoa powder, bicarbonate of soda and salt. Fold half of the dry ingredients into the butter mixture.

4 Mix in the buttermilk, then add the remainder of the dry ingredients and mix until fully incorporated.

5 Using a piping (pastry) bag fitted with a large plain nozzle, pipe 12 5cm/2in rounds of cake mixture (batter) 5cm/2in apart on each baking tray. Bake for 12–15 minutes, or until the cakes bounce back when pressed. Transfer to a wire rack to cool.

6 Meanwhile, and only when you are ready to serve the whoopie pies, remove the ice cream from the freezer, measure it into a bowl or container and leave it to soften for 10 minutes.

7 Using an ice cream scoop, place a scoopful of ice cream on to the flat side of one cake and top with the flat side of another. Smooth the edge of the ice cream with a knife. Repeat to make 12 pies. Drizzle melted chocolate over the tops and decorate with sprinkles.

Energy 367kcal/1549kJ; Protein 6g; Carbohydrate 52g, of which sugars 32g; Fat 17g, of which saturates 10g; Cholesterol 53mg; Calcium 119mg; Fibre 0.9g; Sodium 387mg.

Ice Cream Sandwich Whoopie Pies

These whoopie pies are the perfect indulgence on a hot summer's day. Filled with chocolate ice cream, they should be assembled just before serving. They look fantastic when dipped in melted chocolate, but this can be a race against time before the ice cream melts!

Makes 12 Whoopie Pies

125g/4¼oz/8½ tbsp unsalted butter, softened
175g/6oz/¾ cup light brown sugar
seeds of 1 vanilla pod (bean)
1 egg
350g/12oz/3 cups plain (all-purpose) flour
7.5ml/1½ tsp bicarbonate of soda (baking soda)
5ml/1 tsp salt
250ml/8fl oz/1 cup buttermilk

For the filling and topping
400ml/14fl oz/1⅔ cups chocolate ice cream
100g/3¾oz milk chocolate, melted
unsweetened cocoa powder, to decorate

1 Preheat the oven to 180°C/350°F/Gas 4. Line two baking trays with baking parchment or silicone mats.

2 For the cakes, whisk the butter, brown sugar and vanilla seeds together until light and fluffy. Whisk in the egg. In a separate bowl, sift the flour with the bicarbonate of soda and salt. Fold half of the dry ingredients into the butter mixture. Mix in the buttermilk, then the remaining dry ingredients.

3 Using a piping (pastry) bag fitted with a large plain nozzle, pipe 12 5cm/2in rounds of cake mixture (batter) 5cm/2in apart on each of the baking trays. Bake for 12–15 minutes, or until the cakes bounce back when gently pressed. Transfer to a wire rack to cool.

4 Meanwhile, and only when you are ready to serve the whoopie pies, remove the ice cream from the freezer, measure it into a bowl or container and leave it to soften for 10 minutes.

5 Place a scoopful of ice cream on to the flat side of one cake and top with the flat side of another. Gently squeeze the cakes together. Repeat, working quickly, to make 12 pies. Dip a side of each pie into the melted chocolate, or trickle chocolate over one side, and dust with cocoa powder.

Energy 327kcal/1384kJ; Protein 5g; Carbohydrate 57g, of which sugars 37g; Fat 11g, of which saturates 7g; Cholesterol 45mg; Calcium 78mg; Fibre 0.9g; Sodium 379mg.

Matcha Whoopie Pies

For green tea fanatics, these whoopie pies are a delight with their antioxidant properties. They are also a show-stopper due to their bright green colour. Decorate the edges of the sticky marshmallow with sprinkles for a fun look.

Makes 12 Whoopie Pies

130g/4½oz/generous ½ cup unsalted butter, softened
150g/5oz/¾ cup caster (superfine) sugar
seeds of 1 vanilla pod (bean)
1 egg
325g/11½oz/scant 3 cups plain (all-purpose) flour
7.5ml/1½ tsp bicarbonate of soda (baking soda)
5ml/1 tsp salt
30ml/2 tbsp matcha green tea powder
150ml/5 fl oz/⅔ cup buttermilk
50ml/2fl oz/¼ cup milk

For the marshmallow filling
50ml/2fl oz/¼ cup boiling water
15ml/1 tbsp powdered gelatine
175g/6oz/generous ¾ cup caster (superfine) sugar
75ml/2½fl oz/⅓ cup golden (light corn) syrup
25ml/1½ tbsp cold water
multicoloured sprinkles, to decorate

1 Preheat the oven to 180°C/350°F/Gas 4. Line two baking trays with baking parchment or silicone mats.

2 For the the cakes, beat the butter, sugar and vanilla seeds together until light and creamy. Beat in the egg.

3 In a separate bowl, sift the flour with the bicarbonate of soda, salt and matcha powder. Fold half of the dry ingredients into the butter mixture. Mix in the buttermilk and milk, then the remainder of the dry ingredients.

4 Using a piping (pastry) bag fitted with a large plain nozzle, pipe 12 5cm/2in rounds of cake mixture (batter) 5cm/2in apart on each baking tray. Bake for 12–15 minutes, or until the cakes bounce back when gently pressed. Transfer to a wire rack to cool.

5 To make the filling, place the boiling water in the bowl of an electric mixer and sprinkle with the powdered gelatine. Whisk on low speed until the gelatine dissolves. Set aside. In a deep pan, mix the sugar, golden syrup and cold water together and heat until the mixture comes to a rolling boil, stirring. With the electric mixer still on low speed, gradually pour the hot sugar syrup into the mixing bowl containing the gelatine mixture.

6 Turn the electric mixer to high speed and whisk for about 5 minutes or until the mixture is very thick, pale and fluffy.

7 Spread a tablespoonful of filling on to the flat side of one cake and top with the flat side of another. Repeat to make 12 pies. Roll the edges of the marshmallow in sprinkles.

Energy 308kcal/1305kJ; Protein 4g; Carbohydrate 53g, of which sugars 33g; Fat 10g, of which saturates 6g; Cholesterol 45mg; Calcium 68mg; Fibre1.0g; Sodium 341mg.

Cardamom and Clove Whoopie Pies

Ground spices combine to give an earthy flavour to these delicious whoopies. The spice flavours infuse even more a few days after baking! These whoopies are given a fun 'butterfly' finish, and you could use this technique on any of the recipes in the book.

Makes 9 Whoopie Pies

125g/4½oz/8½ tbsp unsalted butter, softened
175g/6oz/¾ cup light brown sugar
seeds of 1 vanilla pod (bean)
1 egg
350g/12oz/3 cups plain (all-purpose) flour
7.5ml/1½ tsp bicarbonate of soda (baking soda)
5ml/1 tsp salt
5ml/1 tsp ground cardamom
1.5ml/¼ tsp ground cloves
250ml/8fl oz/1 cup buttermilk

For the filling

200ml/7fl oz/1 cup double (heavy) cream
40g/1½oz/3 tbsp caster (superfine) sugar
2.5ml/½ tsp ground cardamom
0.75ml/⅛ tsp ground cloves
icing (confectioners') sugar and ground cinnamon, for dusting

1 Preheat the oven to 180°C/350°F/Gas 4. Line two baking trays with baking parchment or silicone mats.

2 For the cakes, beat the butter, sugar and vanilla seeds together until light and creamy. Add the egg and beat until fully incorporated.

3 In a separate bowl, sift the flour with the bicarbonate of soda, salt, cardamom and cloves.

4 Fold half of the dry ingredients into the butter mixture. Mix in the buttermilk, then the remainder of the dry ingredients.

5 Using a piping (pastry) bag fitted with a large plain nozzle, pipe 12 5cm/2in rounds of cake mixture (batter) 5cm/2in apart on each baking tray. Bake for 12–15 minutes, or until the cakes bounce back when gently pressed. Transfer to a wire rack to cool.

6 Whip the filling ingredients together until stiff peaks form. Using a piping bag fitted with a star-shaped nozzle, pipe some filling on to the flat side of one cake and top with the flat side of another. Repeat to make 9 pies.

7 Dust the pies with icing sugar and cinnamon. There will be 6 spare cakes and some filling remaining. Cut 3 edges off each cake to create 18 'butterfly wings'. Discard (or eat!) the triangles in the centre. Put a spoonful of the remaining filling on each pie and arrange 2 'wings' on top. Dust with more icing sugar and cinnamon.

Energy 455kcal/1911kJ; Protein 5g; Carbohydrate 56g, of which sugars 27g; Fat 25g, of which saturates 15g; Cholesterol 89mg; Calcium 119mg; Fibre 1.5g; Sodium 440mg.

Giant Whoopie Birthday Cake

This supersized whoopie pie makes a perfect birthday cake with its rich chocolate filling and domed top. This recipe produces a very moist sponge, which has an intense chocolate flavour. Alternatives to the dark chocolate topping include whipped cream or chocolate buttercream.

Serves 8 – 10

125g/4¼oz/8½ tbsp unsalted butter, softened
90g/3½oz/scant ½ cup light brown sugar
90g/3½oz/½ cup caster (superfine) sugar
1 egg, beaten
seeds of 1 vanilla pod (bean)
300g/11oz/2¾ cups plain (all-purpose) flour
50g/2oz unsweetened cocoa powder
5ml/1 tsp bicarbonate of soda (baking soda)
5ml/1 tsp salt
250ml/8fl oz/1 cup buttermilk

For the filling and topping
500ml/17fl oz/generous 2 cups double (heavy) cream
75g/3oz/6 tbsp caster (superfine) sugar
seeds of 1 vanilla pod (bean)
65g/2½oz unsweetened cocoa powder
200g/7oz dark (bittersweet) chocolate, melted

1   Preheat the oven to 180°C/350°F/Gas 4. Line two baking trays with baking parchment or silicone mats.

2   For the cakes, beat the butter and sugars together until light and creamy. Beat in the egg, then stir in the vanilla seeds. In a separate bowl, sift the flour with the cocoa powder, bicarbonate of soda and salt.

3   Fold half of the dry ingredients into the butter mixture. Mix the buttermilk in, then the rest of the dry ingredients.

4   Place the collar of a 24cm/9½in springform tin (pan) on to the first baking tray and spoon half of the cake mixture (batter) into the collar, spreading the cake mixture evenly. Remove the collar and repeat the process on the second baking tray. Bake for 15–20 minutes, or until the cakes bounce back when pressed. Transfer to a wire rack to cool.

5   For the filling, whip the cream with the sugar and vanilla seeds until stiff peaks form. Fold in the cocoa powder.

6   Spoon all of the filling on to the flat side of one cake to form a thick layer, spreading evenly. Gently place the other cake on top, flat side down.

7   Pour the melted chocolate over the top of the giant whoopie pie and spread it evenly with a palette knife or metal spatula, allowing it to drip down the side. Serve the cake in slices.

Energy 697kcal/2915kJ; Protein 8g; Carbohydrate 66g, of which sugars 42g; Fat 46g, of which saturates 29g; Cholesterol 123mg; Calcium 130mg; Fibre 1.1g; Sodium 456mg.

Index